Appalachian Dreams

by Jack Trammell

Jack Trammell

Original title
Appalachian Dreams
a bouquet of chapbooks:
Appalachian Dreams - Jack Trammell
Beyond the County Line - Jack Trammell
Belle Isle - Jack Trammell & Audrie Miller

Cover design
Sonja Smolec

Layout & Edit
Sonja Smolec
Yossi Faybish

Published by
Aquillrelle

Copyright 2011
All rights reserved - © Jack Trammell

No part of this book may be reproduced or transmitted in any form or by any means graphic, electronic, or mechanical, including photocopying, recording, taping, or by any information storage retrieval system without the permission, in writing, of the publisher.

ISBN 978-1-105-29646-8

Foreword

Most of these poems were written in the last year or two. I didn't give dates for them simply because they are collected more by feeling than place in time. Some of these were written or published as long ago as 1989. Some of them were written literally as this book was written. I hope the overall flavor is what the title implies.

Special thanks go to my family, and to all those who have followed my writing career with any interest and/or support.

Table of Contents

APPALACHIAN DREAMS

1950 13
Advice 15
Monday Morning 16
getting older 17
sECURITY 18
The Indian Giver 21
Homecoming 22
I Sing For America 23
Mountain 24
Gardening 25
My Window 26
Seeds of Change 28
Old Mill 29
Winter Haiku 30
Divorce 31
Sedition 32
The Day John Parke Fell Asleep 34
imagination 36
Regret 37
The Cedar 38
Jesse 39
Old Man River 40

For You 41
Sandy Creek 42
Fishing 45
God's Calendar Book 46

BEYOND THE COUNTY LINE

Reply to Whitman (and the German Spiritualist) 53
What would Cicero Say? 54
Stress 56
D.Z.'s Subjects 57
The County Boundary 58
Colors 59
Five Days Traveling on the James River from the 60
Muddy Creek (Day#1) 61
Herring Creek (Day #2) 62
Confluence of the James and Chickahominy (Day#3) 64
Chippokes Beach (Day#4) 65
Lower James (Day#5) 66
The Potomac 67
Garden Diary 1999 68
Jesse's Plow 70
The Girl in Whitley City 71
Future Trend 72
I've Seen Your Stormy Seas 73
Capuchin Creek 74
Sermon on Stephens Knob 75

Butternut Sky 76
Those Who Came Before Me 77
Humpback Mountain 78
The Great Trout Strike of '99 80
Man with a Fiddle 82
Aroma 83
North Marsh Creek 84
Ode to Cleopatra 85
When I Saw the Great Impressionists 86
Emily 87
Reflections on Stalingrad 88
Grandma's Bread 90
Yellow Rose 92
Oasis 93
Edgar Poe 94

Belle Isle

Dear Turkey, Happy Day 101
Man is Born to Fish 102
Turkey Day 2, 3, 4, 5 103
Beauty Fades 106
Simple Riddle 107
The Great Wall of Japan 108
Blue Days When the Sun Goes Down 109
Rhyming Game 110
Dancer's New Song 112

Early Morning Light 113
Hairy France 114
Season Change 115
Kid Quotes 116
Ode to Ned 118
Mrs. Greenhow 120
Mind of the Terrorist 121
Haiku 122
A New One 123
Discovery (Crabtree Falls at Night) 124
New Color 125
Boys Like Trains 126
Coming off the Mountain 128
Falling in Love (Again) 129
Fernandina Beach 130
Child's Question 131
Rising Action 132
Asklepios 133
List 03/19/02 at Urkops 134
Mission on Three Ridges 135
Waking Up By the River 136
The Heart! 137
That Faraway Place 138
By the Laughing Ocean 139
Summer Storm 140
Sleepless in Bumpass 141

Coffee House Blues	142
Prayer #1	145
Reminder	146
Hannah, My Hannah	147
Drunken Fella	148
From Amos to Audrie	151
Before Me	152
Trial and Error	153
Lament #7	154
My Gift to You	156
The Poe Syndrome (journal entry dated 1841)	158
Birds and Bees	160
Sweet Sun Rays	161
Marsh Creek	162
A Shape I Wist	163
Portrait of a Shipwreck	164
Diversity	166
Portrait of A.	167
Jack's Bad Day	168
Spider	169
Another Battle	170
Garden Haiku	171
Lucky	172
1990 and The Promise	173
Poet's Advice	174
Loss	175

The Zebra Finch Revolt 176
Old House 177
Life of the Poet 178
The Miller's Wife (A poddle, or a poem that is also a riddle)... 179
Get There 180
Romania 182
The End 183
Psalm #231 184
Prayer #15 185
Cantos XVII 186
Aging 188
Trackside 189
The Fight 190
About Christmas 191

Appalachian Dreams

Jack Trammell

Appalachian Dreams is devoted to the notion that where we come from geographically has a profound impact on who we are, and especially, who we might become in an imaginary future. My birthplace was in the mountains of eastern Kentucky, and though my path has taken me many places far away, the existence of that place is an existence that far outweighs my own transient stay on earth.

These poems, and fragments of images that poetry cannot penetrate, are about more than just Kentucky, though, or Appalachia in general--they are about technology's sudden takeover, the loss of God, the loss of nature and its appreciation, the loss of historical perspective, and many other complexities of modern life.

And above all, they are poems of someone from Appalachia trying to reconcile simplicity with inexplicability. I was born on the west side of the mountains, and now reside on the east side of them, but these thoughts, and also my heart, continue to roam somewhere in-between, where mysteries and great beauties still remain, waiting patiently to be appreciated.

1950

small county,
        BIG COUNTRY.
doors locked at night
        to let in the land.

people smiled more then
        i should wish at me,
because i'd freeze it and
        jealously keep them hidden.

the time is gone and
        my heart aches so...
deep, pending reality pains
        strike chords of resentment.

what do men know?
        saying that time is relative!
that nothing ever changes,
        as if rain doesn't level furrows.

the small people living
        small lives,
hot nights, with broken screens,
        1950.

i close my eyes and
        i can taste it!
i missed my chance,
        tragically, i missed it...

Jack Trammell

these people were for me, as
    roots outlive the leaves
lonely train whistles signal
    melancholy season changes.

i missed it.
    the smell lingers
in the air like some
    musty forgotten attic.

i missed it,
    didn't even exist
couldn't possibly understand
    what i didn't live.

but i do understand.
    my grandparents, still,
live in these places,
    and i will too.

somehow!
1950.

I envy the simple life my grandparents lived in the 1950s raising my father and uncle. Many days I wish I could raise my children in a world like that.

Advice

The Old man has memories.
                     I have fresh marks.
                     Wounds from the world.

His advice:
    "Slow down
           Until you can hear
the insects buzzing near the porch."

From his perch he has seen
The Ways of the World,
Watched flies land on the warm brick
Then disappear in the hazy heat.

He has tilled the ground
And studied the people
That will someday return to
Heaven dirt.

He says:
    "In life
           You must heal your wounds,
But keep all of your memories."

The old man has his memories.
                     I have yet to find them,
                     My wounds heal so slowly.

This old man can still be seen sitting on his porch, if you happen to drive by the right house in Cumberland territory.

Monday Morning

Sick, angry feeling in the pit of my stomach
Laced with a lack of sleep and cognizance...
I go from loved ones to not so loved ones,
To those who are just as angry themselves.

There is this notion in my mind that a thing is wrong
If it always feels so contrary to human nature...
So I despise this ugly morning
Which soon is just a forgotten memory.

I reject that good must start with bad,
Or that all good things must come to an end.
Instead why not get at the heart,
And do away with it all together?

(to be continued...)

getting older

Getting older is like
imagination.
The discovery of things never conceived
or nightmared.

The oldest person on earth
The biggest imagination
The youngest person on earth
the smallest dream.

I feel some aches
And I discover some pains
But I wonder if it really signals
some new status thing.

I can't conceive of what's next?
Every physical lasso twirls
The mists of confusion melt away
death understands death.

Stare aging in the eye
You will see no reflection
You change so fast, age so rapidly
it's gone by then; lost.

Jack Trammell

sECURITY

what we really have to thank the romans for
litigation
199? what?
counting single raindrops as they fall down

over 100,000 new BOOKS enter the world
marching like spartan soldiers
trained to fight
illiterate goose-stepping fire ants

AND the medium may be the message
internet trash
10,000 new web sites a day
new ideas like the dodo bird

truth sweet god's breath
lost, now that "violence is fine"
if arthur is taken out of context
murder is a vote

AND the greeks gave us philosophy
but forgot to include instructions
we supply the batteries
and create the WWW sites

security is a rocket about to be launched
out of inner space
into a second middle age
while the Pope wonders where exactly he lost control

199? the age of unreason
great literature = great television
ezra pound + charles dickens = cnn
"at behest of usura"

crying babies scream for their mother's
or warmth
or milk
or a good dime-store novel you can read in an afternoon

security is a blanket
run through the laundry once too many
times, spare change in the
age of the timid

AND a child comes with questions
browned Torah, Koran, BIBLE, Tripitaka, Veda
SEND EM' TO THE WEB SITE
page 652 world almanac

a thief comes prowling in the night
security is electronic impulses
"the desire for safety"
tacitus wrote about history, not burglars

shame on us
199? looking at single raindrops
through electron microscopes while
THE THIEF IS AT THE DOOR

will cnn cover the next world war?
if anyone will volunteer to organize it
perhaps no one will show up
but the button pushers and politicians

Jack Trammell

AND security is not a company
or a state of mind
or a foreign policy
OR A **&%$# WWW (site)

security is a lock on your door
a hasp on your intellect
a single raindrop
somewhere off the phone lines

an idea that is still original
a book that hasn't been written yet
a child not born yet
a monkey sitting at his typewriter, still

creating plots diluted
watered down to flaccid gutter rinse
only people are cheap
words are just affordable

AND what does it mean
but 199? will pass into papyrus
and security will change
SPELL IT WITH A CAPITAL LETTER

(first published in 'Word Salad' in 1997)

The Indian Giver

The Indian Giver built his house on sand,
Treading where angels fear to fly.
He fought in wars before I was born,
Which he recounted on a cracked checkerboard.
He wooed countless beauties,
Remembering each one with a twinkle in his eyes.
He knew every wives tale,
Some he invented on his own.

Years later, I found him again,
I was so jealous of the new youth at his table.
I found myself indignant,
When he barely mustered a lazy wave in my direction.
I felt so out of place,
That I quickly left in thoughtful consternation.
Somehow I felt cheated, though I wasn't sure why,
After all, the checkerboard had always been his.

(published in 'Wide Open Magazine'; finalist in contest)

Jack Trammell

Homecoming

Feel the breeze on my face; smell the cedar wood burning;
Watch the golden rod waving in the constant, gentle wind.
The sound of water running echoes through a hackberry hollow,
While opossums, copperheads, deer watch me perform my tests.

The grass really is blue, melding into a concave sky,
Soaking up the march sunlight like a sponge collecting water.
I cut locust posts, and drag them through the dusty hills,
Building a strong, rustic fence around the things that I love.

Cattle graze, ill-bred, unaware of the ground they trample,
So recently sanctified by the blood of indians and pioneers.
Red-tinged dirt, maybe crimson life fluids stain it yet,
Growing grass so strong that it blooms at mere hints of rain.

This land I was born in calls me back with the hoot of an owl,
Caressing me from afar with the soft touch of river waters.
My roots stretch out, far into fertile soil, reaching,
Seeking out the nutrients, life, love and soul of home.

(first published in the 'Fauquier Poetry Journal')

I Sing For America

Walt Whitman
Knew
The Stars and Stripes,
He knew the swing of the ax,
The way the blade cuts down to create
Startling new shapes and forms.

Like a thunder
Storm
Brewing, he knew the storm's hiss,
The trill of the foreman's horn,
Signaling the end of a shift
In human thought and progress.

My America was his
America
Growing, living, thriving, hurting,
With wicked men and hearty women,
Wanting so badly to succeed that
Success has become part of the very dirt.

Walt Whitman
Knew
His America is my America,
The worst of his generation,
Like doves in an age of poetless workers
Still ring the bells loud and clear--America!

(first published in the 'Fauquier Poetry Journal')

Jack Trammell

Mountain

A mountain
Is not a mountain
Until you stand at its summit.

And discover that it was made to see inside the distance.

Gardening

Dirt
what we call people
What we all come from
what we all go to.

Growing things is like
growing God in dirt
Nurturing, watching, waiting
hoping the rain doesn't fall hard.

The sun gives life
then takes it away
Blazing like some constant
alien ray gun.

Plants wither, sometimes
bearing fruit even after death
Like some closeted writer
discovered in a basement box.

The garden is where
realization struck me like a plow hitting a rock
A man can't help but be humble
if he grows.

Humility, a flower and a fruit.

Jack Trammell

My Window

1.   I have my own window
    That looks out on space
    Occupied by winter colors,
    Countryside unmasked by cold
    Valley with no river running
    Simply ground where rain dances.

2.   The window is my light
    Allowing sun warmth in;
    Night cold steals later;
    Always an open page
    To write what I see
    What I feel.

3.   Every morning Christmas
    Gifts of nuts and leaves
    Dead grass between white oaks
    Where squirrels run
    Frightened by my face
    Along brittle branches.

4.   At night the hills flatten,
    Stretching out to distant towns
    Where men plan small wars,
    Battle intended to restore
    The lost sense of hope
    In an epoch of new found certainty.

5. But the light restores me,
Draws up trees and hills
To surround me with hope,
Burrows under my foundations,
Shoring them up
For the day to come.

Wendell Berry is recognized as a great Kentucky writer of "clarity and sureness." His poetry reflects the importance of place, and specifically central Kentucky. This poem is simply a tribute to him.

Seeds of Change

Seeds of change are sown in the breeze
To tumble with invisible whirlwinds.
Scattering from one end of the earth to the other
They ruffle the harbinger crows.

They bounce and they bound, swirling like leaves
Knocking ever so faintly on the glass.
And innocent people throw their windows wide open
Only to let the unsuspected trouble in.

(Published in two 1989 collections)

Old Mill

Faint plinking of paddle piercing clear water
Drowned out by grumbling rapids,
Old Mill emerges
Hushing spring-bare ashes and beech.

We make camp at the base of it, Ross and I,
Marveling that forty feet walls of hewn stone
Need no steel.
Silhouette against a graying twilight,
Old keep running beside an even older road,
A wren lights in a window frame and
    I fear the whole structure will crumble...
But it only tries the silence.

A sign read "No Trespassing"
    (For the living)
Dare we venture inside?
Old graves nearby, piles of river-washed stones
Arranged so the future will recognize the past.
Here a chalk bone, too large to be human?
Maybe bovine; pelvic, or some Jurassic
Period time effect fallen off the pallet.

Quiet crackle of fire singing in cold air
Punctured by night owl and sleepy rapids,
Old Mill a sentinel,
Whispering two-hundred-year-old dream/ghosts.

(published in the 'Fauquier Poetry Journal') The Slate River is a beautiful, historic, isolated stretch of Virginia water that pushes into the James River near Bremo Bluff. During high spring waters, canoeing is excellent.

Jack Trammell

Winter Haiku

House on winter hill
Siding turning one color
Native soil and mud.

Single blade of grass
Resting unconscious alone
Spring inside of it.

Old oak tree so tall
Branches bare and angry so
Old part of the land.

Rain in the air
Smell of country wet earth ground
Dampness windborn sound.

Light inside the house
Glowing like summer fire flies
Warming the country.

(these Haiku appeared in a school journal) Winter is the season for all seasons in Virginia, combining rain, snow, sleet, sunshine, thunderstorms, bleak grey clouds, and bitter-cold wood-burning days. It's a time that's never quite what we want it to be.

Divorce

Sometimes I dream
With my eyes closed,
And I can see the
Sports and dots that color life.

I see people and pets
And things that I want to do,
In a slow motion movie
That never pauses or rewinds.

In my dreams
It's spring time,
Where buds are blooming
And families are together.

I play for the Falcons,
I sing in a band,
I captain the Enterprise,
And I don't feel any pain at all.

Jack Trammell

Sedition

Part I -- pray to God, for
Strength to live inside this empty shell;
Pray for comfort instead of answers.
Let your liberalism bleed you to
Death... Slowly.

The crime is sedition.
The race is not to the finish
But rather to outpace your outer garments;
The race of the Hollow Men.

A man cannot be God.
God is too thick.

A man's heart, though, is dense
Like the core of a neutron star
So packed with "things"
That the beginnings of truth are like
Cosmic dust dancing in the sunlight.

Part II -- beg for mercy, for
Strength to shed the outer hull;
Pray for the answers, ---- you!
We all want to know why
Why... Quickly!

The crime was sedition.
The race has already been run
Past the finish line into history;
A list of genocidal generals and pious praetors.

A man can be a god.
So think in certain places.

A man's heart, then, is heavy
Dragged down by gravity and graveness
So stuffed with "things"
That the end of truth is a joke
Which only the criminal can atone for.

(published in 'GrePerry', an on-line journal) People always seem to forget the charge officially brought against Him. The Romans were not dumb--they had a law that covered every situation, including one that could deal with a Messiah.

The Day John Parke Fell Asleep

At 5:15 a whistle blows and
The rails begin to shake.
At 5:15 the air clouds with smoke
The express is running late.
At 5:15, John Parke sits, leaning on the throttle.
At 5:15, John Parke sits, leaning on the throttle.

At 5:16 the crossing gates
Slam down at Darby Junction.
At 5:16 boys congregate
Waving caps in dull slow motion.
At 5:16, John Parke sits, his eyelids growing heavy.
At 5:16, John Parke sits, his eyelids growing heavy.

At 5:18 the brakeman calls
To check the old girl's speed.
At 5:18 he tries to call
But Parke pays the phone no heed.
At 5:18, John Parke sits, and doesn't hear the phone.
At 5:18, John Parke sits, and doesn't hear the phone.

At 5:22 the alarm spreads out
Tapped out in terse Morse Code.
At 5:22 there is no doubt
It's a runaway carrying full load.
At 5:22, John Parke sits, snoring in his seat.
At 5:22, John Parke sits, snoring in his seat.

At 5:27 the train gains speed
Heading down the old cut in the hill.
At 5:27 every old-timer can see

At Grant's curve there'll be a great spill.
At 5:27, John Parke sits, rubbing the sleep from his eyes
At 5:27, John Parke sits, rubbing the sleep from his eyes.

At 5:30 exactly, remember it well,
That train sailed right off the tracks.
At 5:30 exactly, Parke rang the old bell
For the express would never come back.
At 5:30, John Parke sits, hoping the brakeman cut loose.
At 5:30, John Parke sits, smiling--for what else could he do?

Jack Trammell

imagination

imagination

is the invention
of things that really
exist in a vacuum

where we look to find
doors leading into
the center of joy

everything's possible
because love is money
stable currency of life

where wildest dreamensions
cool nothings
and two hearts share blood

and nothing
is impossible
likely

(first published in 1996 in the 'New Author's Journal')

Regret

Feelings are like gossamer threads, fragile webs stretched
Tightly between a rose and a thorn bush in the wilderness.

Men tramp off to war, unaware of the silky hair that
Clings to their muddy boots and pant cuffs.

(first published in 1991)

Jack Trammell

The Cedar

The Cedar line the hills, sprouting up like day old stubble
Branches and limbs so very silent.
With a color like ghost green, as if they never see the sun
They claim neither winter nor summer.

They creep upon the fields, when eyes are turned away
Blotting the vibrancy of pasture.
They clog thickest woods, ford the deepest of streams
Mourning at all of nature's funerals.

What a plain, ordinary tree (or is it just a shrub?)
Never to be rose or weeping willow.
But men will pass away, and their fields will go unplowed
The Cedar will remain among the ruins.

(1989 'Sparrowgrass Poetry Forum')

Jesse

Jesse came from the mountains
    Naked in the cold rain
Happy,
    Was known as a poet-laureate.

I followed his words
    Like sand eroding
Monuments,
    Best friend I never had.

I feel as if I should have known him
    Like the nape of my back
Never
    Did I lay eyes upon him.

There is another thing I know
    No shadow of a doubt
This,
    He knew me very well.

(first published in 1989)

Jack Trammell

Old Man River

He was an innocent bystander,
A lost soul creeping toward obscurity,
A cold heart crushed in the currents.

Barges still pass over his place
Without a nod or smile;
Just a lonely flask offered in peace.

Deer graze along the banks and
Their pricked ears hear his whisper,
Causing them to scatter to the fields.

The trees on the hills
They know why he is there,
But they promised not to tell a soul.

(published first in 'TelStar')

For You

When I walk in winter, I feel less Grey;
I walk on pine cone Paths;
I know the way to Eden.

Should I rejoice in this salt-less Season?

Breath deeply of the future;
Feel veins pump blood into our living hearts;
Drink a timeless toast with me to ruby red,

    Razor-sharp,

        On pins and needles,

            Life.

(for a very special person I care about--first published in 'Fauquier Poetry Journal')

Jack Trammell

Sandy Creek
a three part journey

Part 1

The unknowing call it a swamp
Environmentalists,
                                    haughtysyncophants
Call it a wetland.

A place can be a haven for
Things,
                                    humansensabilities
Assume snakes, irises, oaks.

Sanctuary in a shrinking habitat
Places,
                                    quietescapisms
To hear the buzz of a deerfly.

People lam out from city places
Folks,
                                    misunderstandophants
Smiling stupid at blooms.

I hear and feel the swamp
Living,
                                    ignoringme
I breath it in like perfume.

Part 2

The river runs through the swamp,
Right where the water lilies smile at sunshine
Beavers timber trees they can't possibly
Understand why.

Fish run cool, dark and silver in lazy rapids,
Emotionless until a frightened moment
Black reel buzzes and bends and bears
Heavy weight of struggle.

A pickerel, rows of sharp teeth,
Freshwater alligator of shallow cools
Helpless in a fiberglass canoe
While two students of nature learn afresh.

We smile and the river smiles back,
Pointing those who question to secrets
Within old stones, the ruins of a mill
Clothed in vines before naked water.

Then a curve, around the edge of one universe,
Into another dimension
Where time is a watch that keeps hesitating
Each second a little longer/shorter than next.

Part 3

Night beside the lakes is a stranger shade of green:
A place where weary navigators and owls quietly preen.

A place where sleeping rocks and dozing hemlock dream:
A place that traps the moonlight and crowns it virgin queen.

Words become like silence,
    Of which you never drink your fill

To quench the evil human violence,
    That pollutes our purest thrill.

The silence bliss.
It tucks you in.

God's kiss.
Washes sin.

Reprise

When the morning returns, we trek back to the city.

Fishing

Come with me to my favorite white oak
Where the secrets of nature are revealed.
The swirl of the trout, and the gurgling brook
Are the language whispered in the air.

The rustling leaves provide the percussion
For a symphony of natural celebration.
The sunlight, filtering through them
Provides a sparkling light show in tandem.

Join me, and bring your string and stick.
With a sharp brass hook, and a bit of luck,
You can catch the very essence of life
And take it home for dinner.

God's Calendar Book

"I'll pencil you in for Friday--maybe. Let me check."

You see, Monday I've got this
Fertile Crescent situation going.
Assyrians are coming over for dinner and
the place is a mess.

Tuesday's no better
Got Legions and sickos with crowns
Running around and I'm to stay at home and
watch the new alarm system be installed.

On Wednesday you've got
Crusades! (and I hear it's in my NAME)
I wish those guys would let me
catch up on some damn paperwork.

Thursday, unfortunately, I promised
The artists the Renaissance
(How many hundreds of years to figure our perspective?) and
I have to make a cameo appearance.

Friday, actually, I see now the
Americans--I promised them a little
Tiny bit of vanity.
And I suppose I should watch it on t.v.

What about Saturday?
It's all I've got left,
You see Sunday is out of the question.
And I assume that you'll want me to be there???

Beyond the County Line
Jack Trammell

Beyond the County Line is meant to be a sequel to the collection of poetry that appeared in 1997 under the title of Appalachian Dreams.

It represents a much shorter time frame than the previous collection, however, and it is probably different in several other ways, as well, that the reader will probably notice. Where appropriate, reference to previous publication is made.

I hope these songs bring some moments of enjoyment to my readers.

"I forget how many thousand eggs go wrong for one codfish that gets hatched. But as Berkeley said long ago, it is idle to censure the creation as wasteful if you believe in a creator who has unlimited stuff to play with."

--Sir Frederick Pollock

"At an early age on one of my walks in the Kentucky hills I thought a great thought... It was this: People last only a short time. Nature plays a trick on them. She stays young forever."

--Jesse Stuart

Reply to Whitman (and the German Spiritualist)

Some things are really lost,
Some identities, forms, and objects of the world,
Some are lost forever.
Never to return.

That look that passes between lovers;
The smell of Hiroshima five minutes afterwards;
Some things are really lost.

The color of the sky above Auschwitz;
The pitiful, dying moans of Julius Caesar;
Some things are really lost.

The funeral dirge chanted by a mother;
The snap of the yellow tape at the finish line;
Some things are really lost.

The great library at Alexandria;
The exact moment you realize you're an adult;
Some things are really lost.

Some things are really lost,
With all due respects to poet and philosopher,
Some are lost forever.
Never to return.

Jack Trammell

What would Cicero Say?

What would Cicero say
If he looked at us closely today?

Would he have his own glitzy web site?
Would he treat all computers as a blight?

Would he run for a seat in Congress?
Or would he be another Clinton appointee that dies in confirmation hearings...

"These kids these days..." he might say,
Smiling all the while and waving to the cameras.

"Political Correctness was our invention," he might claim,
Muttering: "If I'd only known the Christians were coming..."

What would Cicero say today
If he saw the ruins of Pompeii?

"The tourists take pictures of the dead?"
Touring Rwanda, Bosnia and Washington D.C.

"How long until I get to see the President?" he might say.
"Your place in history failed by one vote," the Republicans would say.

What would Cicero say today
If he saw the books we display?

"I thought paper would change the world," he might say.
Limping through the halls of a chaotic school.

"I thought the Roman Legacy might survive
Somewhere besides Ezra Pound."

And Cicero would return to history very sadly,
But with his tongue pierced
His soul saved
And a Visa/Master Card in the folds of his toga.

(appeared in the 'Fauquier Poetry Journal' October 1998)

Stress

Sometimes you don't even notice it.
The possibility doesn't even occur to you.
Realization aches at awkward moments.
Entire days can vanish in its wake.
Sometimes you don't even notice it.
Strength must be sought in strong places.

D.Z.'s Subjects

Mountain laurel, green umbrella
Leaves cupped with snow.
Mountain stream, ice-lipped
Water colds and frozen rocks.
Brooding stag, shoulders rippling
Sinews alert with poise.
Thick brush under shadow
Leaves clinging to sienna oaks.
Snow silent, everywhere quiet
Covering vivid green pines.
Smoke, lazy and sleepy
Crawling toward heaven slowly.
Hunter's back, plaid jacket
Floating through wild sunflowers.

Jack Trammell

The County Boundary

They found the old boundary stones and
Moved the county line a half a mile.

Some cared; some didn't
But no one seemed to question!

Maybe the ancients were wrong,
Maybe the stones were wrong.
It could be the computers were right,
Someone could have moved the old stones.

They moved the county line and
Worshipped rediscovered history.

But no one seemed to question!
Maybe the stones were wrong.

Colors

Autumn is to red and orange as
Renoir is to blue and green.
Spring is to Monet as
Water is to the oceans.

Jack Trammell

Five Days Traveling on the James River from the Appalachian Mountains to the Atlantic

"Man shapes himself through decisions that shape his environment," said bacteriologist René Dubos, and my decision to travel along the James River extensively and support Chesapeake Bay preservation projects has reshaped me in the past two years. No one should make environmental decisions about such beautiful places without first traveling there themselves to study the complex relationships and witness firsthand the beauty of the geology and life forms. These poems are fragments of a much longer journal I keep whenever I travel near or on the bay and its tributaries.

Muddy Creek (Day#1)

Cathedral banks, high and steep,
Attended by stern white oaks and maples,
Music is birdsong, Carolina wren,
And the silence.

Somewhere downstream
Is the James, wide and swift,
Here is Southern patience, however,
And the silence.

Someone speaks and it
Breaks the spell,
Even the tree frogs and crickets
Pause in surprise.

Darters and shiners
Dragonfly nymphs and decaying leaves,
Sunlight pries at brown water
And the silence.

Jack Trammell

Herring Creek (Day #2)

Starts slowly,
Narrow and sluggish
Buzzing muddy with snakes
That stare for long moments.

The birds are rulers
Ignoring everything but fish,
Dusty blue herons; paper white Egrets;
Screeching brownish Osprey.

Unwinds like a string
That grows wider and wider,
Until the murkish water is deep, and
Mud flats squint to see one another.

The fish are the subjects
Ignoring everything but birds,
Nervous silver shad; iridescent spotted shiners;
Spotted flat hogchokers.

Rushes into the arms of the James,
Flat, placid and broad,
Seasoned with salt and brine, and
Flavored with silt.

The plants are the spectators,
Armies of silent biology,
Heart-pickerel weed; Beading never wet;
Tall and spindly wild rice.

Hidden in southern pine and cypress,
Herring Creek laps against the shores of
Shirley Plantation, reptilian haven,
A place where time stands still.

Confluence of the James and Chickahominy (Day #3)

Where one ends
Something else begins,
Indian shadows and pioneer spirits
Co-mingle where waters swirl and mix.

Gray horizon
Touches the James,
Spreading out beyond a rusting wreck
To the far distant misty shore.

Osprey cry and
Yellow ring perch dart,
Which river they're in
Matters little to either of them.

Somewhere between
Warm blankets of water,
There is a marriage, a place
Where one river becomes the other.

The exact spot remains
Hidden and obscure,
Though Lady Rebecca swam there,
Surely she knew where it was.

Chippokes Beach (Day #4)

There is a flat bay with mystery fluidity;
There is lightning jumping close by;
There are cliffs falling off green hills;
There are layers upon layers of lost years.
We anchor the ship, study dismal sky,
Canoes repel the water away from nothing.
The foggy beach is littered with the past's trash:
Shells, bones, fragments of fragments of things.

A little white coral; a blackened whale bone;
All of the rocky harvest from the eroding cliffs
That tells us how young we are, and
How utterly much we will never know.

Tides dominate the small creek,
Exposing fiddler crabs, then obscuring them.
Tall pines, aromatic and sticky, compete with
White oaks to see the dead plantation.

It is a place of peace, and it must have been so
Even thousands of untold years ago.
The giant scallops were as taciturn then
As the brittle, porous fossil remains today.

Lower James (Day#5)

I heard a rumor that
Blue cats had taken it over,
But I found plenty of
Eels, crabs, croakers, spot.

Boat Junkyards and
Rusting ghost battleships
Made a momentary defiance,
But the flatness defeated them.

Six inches deep, or
Sixty fathoms, somehow
It all looked the same, though
The captain could smell it out.

Huge container ships,
Red, black, silent, churning,
Passed silently over oyster beds
While saltiness hit all senses.

Atlantic Ocean, cold
Gray receiver of land spirits,
Gateway to everywhere else,
The conscience of mountains.

There was a parting of ways
At some dock in Newport News,
Where barnacled tugboats watched
And the James finally disappeared.

The Potomac

Muddy insolent, rippling deceptively,
Winding your way to an unlikely capitol.
Are you beautiful? or
Indifferent and dangerous.

Jack Trammell

Garden Diary 1999

As I sit at my desk writing this, I am looking outside at my garden, baking in the hot Memorial Day sun. I can also see beyond the front porch roof to the sky, where ominous dark clouds hint at the possibility of an afternoon shower. It reminds me of how much the struggle to grow this food has dominated my emotions in the past two months.

Disaster: God sent
A plague of dogs
Fighting, rolling, smashing
Greenhouse plants, just set
Broken, flattened, like road kill.

And then he sent a second plague:
Birds, black, cawing,
Picking corn seedlings like men
Pulling cards in a game of poker,
Eating seed remains,
Laughing, until
Scarecrow man joined the game.

And God was still angry, and
Sent a plague of rabbits
Nibble, nibble, little left
Every bean leaf gone, transported,
Stripped bare to the stem:
More seed, more hard ground.

And the dogs returned,
Only this time rocks were exchanged
With the dogs taking the worse of it,
And the gardener praying,
Praying now for rain.

Jack Trammell

Jesse's Plow

I turned over dirt
With the moldboard
Glistening, crumbling,
To discover a new land,
Like Columbus,
A sod of youthful surprise.

The Girl in Whitley City

February
Cold time of longings.
Spring
Begging outside the door.

She was the first half of light, and
I was a poor fraction of the ways of men.

Like the changing seasons
She was never the same person.
When I look at her now
There's some subtle change,
Some shift in the way I perceive her,
Beautiful and primitive.

Her smile was a message to me,
From all the gods who defy death,
Full of final chapters and last good-byes, and
Her heart should have been my mapping star.

That old town, it's
Just another heartbeat on the calendar.

She was the
Second half of light.
Me, now, a
Distant close admirer.

Jack Trammell

Future Trend

What happens? When the subdivision of one city
Collides with one from the next.
Perhaps a new city appears.

What happens? When everyone has a web site
Email addresses, and a lawyer.
Perhaps more communication.

What happens? When population equals resources
Equality no longer a math equation.
Perhaps good will toward men.

What happens? When Human genes become currency
Clones graze where fields were.
Perhaps a better species.

What happens? When a palm-size disc
Holds all of history on it.
Perhaps more understanding.

What happens? When television becomes interactive
People plug in rather than tune in.
Perhaps better entertainment.

The future is bright, is it not? A white, radiant light
So absolutely intense
That it consumes everything

But the blackness.

I've Seen Your Stormy Seas
for AJ

We share a common place, in heart
A hill with rocky brook and trees,
We share another secret, as well,
Deeper than blood and oak roots.

I know your face, know it well,
I see a possibility of contentment,
Your soft intelligence leaves me
Promise of smoothness for asperity.

Your slender hands are like the roads
That wind through Blackbird Hollow,
Along the county line
Near to where you were born.

Holding your hand would be like
Touching a stormy sea, without fear;

Looking into your eyes would be like
Waking from a perfect sleep.

I come from that place, our place,
Know you like the nape of my back.
I feel you dream along that dusty track
Where someday we will touch, together.

Patience, I remind myself,
For the world stretches evil beyond the pale,
Patience, for I feel you approaching,
Perhaps years away, but ever closer.

Jack Trammell

Capuchin Creek

Where I am, and
Where I'm going.
Might as well be a path
Leading to a family field in Capuchin.

Along that trail,
Weaving between shadow mountains and
Ancient white oaks,
I make camp with my memories.

What's the difference?
I wonder...
Between an old family photograph
And my son sleeping beside me.

Shadows close-in, falling
Thoughts of places and rivers,
Homesteads on eroded hills,
Watchtowers of my eternity.

('Poetry Heaven Quarterly', April 2000)

Sermon on Stephens Knob

Has this river really flowed for so long? Or, perhaps,
God made the stones round from the beginning.

Was there ever a time no snakes lived on this mountain?
Or, perhaps, God placed them there when he saw the empty rocks.

Was there a time when these oaks were not here?
Or, perhaps, God placed them in the folds of the earth all along.

Was there a time when your heart was not here?
Or, perhaps, There was just a time when you were too far away.

Butternut Sky

In a butternut sky
Revealed by sunrise,
Night blossoms into blue.

Frozen dew mist
Sleeps in late,
Chilly blanket for white grass.

The county wakes up
Here a man in boots,
There the hum of tires on tar.

Slowly at first,
Then with more vigor,
Butternut sky melds into yellow.

Those Who Came Before Me

I swear an oath of loyalty
To those who came before me.
Generals, heroes and horse thieves alike
I claim you all as kin.

Some of you are hanging frozen
Upon the cabin wall;
Some of you exist quite lonely in
Legend crypts of time.

I swear an oath of loyalty
To those who came before me.
You led the way through mountain passes,
Died in hollows lost to time.

Some of you I know by name,
Some I know by spirit.
The tales are passed from mouth to mouth
And down to generations.

I swear an oath of loyalty
I make a promise firm.
To those who came before me,
Your lives were not in vain.

Jack Trammell

Humpback Mountain

Somewhere in the distance
It rises in the mist.
Not one peak, but
Several summits and a basin,
All covered in sheets of fog.

When the mountain wakes,
A path is revealed
Silent and perfect, leading
Above a thunderstorm
In the valley far below.

Wonders abound:
White oaks, future whiskey barrels,
Mullein, Indian tobacco,
Red Junipers, aromatic spicy scent,
The Calico Bush and the Rosebay.

At the top, old stone walls
Reveal the past, hogpens, and
A farmer's worn footpath,
Leading to the rocks,
Where tourists and savages amble.

Remains of sheer granite cliffs,
Worthy of the Rockies,
Now a pile of worn dominos
Left to tumble downhill,
Markers of human futility.

Below, the gap is still shrouded,
Old Howardsville Turnpike,
Where the settlers sited in
On Humpback Rocks,
Now a dirt path winding nowhere.

Jack Trammell

The Great Trout Strike of '99

My son scared the fish off, with his
Crashing march through the best pools,
Or maybe it was something else, but
No fish were biting.

I found out later the trout were on
Strike, some kind of damn protest against
Excessive pressure on the river and a
Complete utter lack of peace and quiet.

The wildlife rangers kind of laughed about it,
Reminding me, "We'll stock again next week.
The surge of new fish will dilute the
Influence of the trouble-makers."

But what if it spreads? I wondered,
Casting my line listlessly, like a frog
Darting its tongue out for no apparent reason.
What if they all go on strike together?

The rangers wouldn't answer, looking like
Some rich Rockefeller types in green suits.
They left after checking everyone's license
(But do you need one when the fish walk out?)

I cast behind every swirl, let my line
Drift through every favorite rocky lair,
Slung my bait into remote eddies so it
Tumbled through the best crowded channels.

I prayed to the fish gods and
Jealously spied on dozens of competitors,
Blinking when they twitched their lines—
--One person even caught a shiny scab.

The trout, though, I had to concede,
Had one or two gripes I could relate to.
I wouldn't eat half of that stuff, either,
And I certainly hate the crowds on the bank.

My son, he thought the strike was kinda funny,
And I tried to smile about it, too,
Though my creel was empty, Ross said,
"Isn't it a lovely day?"

Jack Trammell

Man with a Fiddle

Black hair swaying over his face
The fiddle player keeps his pace
Arm bouncing up and around, down

Sometimes he grins; sometimes grimaces;
The fiddle is smooth, tenacious,
A musical bourbon whiskey

Banjo, guitar, old bass and uke
Sounds from the hollows, absolute
Heaven bound, to those came before

The bowstring dances like a skinny girl
Country flower with skirts awhirl,
Close my eyes, and I'm home again.

Aroma

Imagine a world without coffee...
It's possible, though
What would I do?
Or a world without chocolate...
As in ancient days, or
Was chocolate in Eden?
A world without computers?
I don't like the smell of that,
Though I can imagine it.
A world without words?
Impossible!
Even nothing has a word.
But a world without coffee, is
A world that waxes superficial,
A world without aroma.

Jack Trammell

North Marsh Creek

Hot summers,
Cold water,
Copperhead dreams
Mixed with black bottom dirt.

Great, great grandfather
Plowed that dirt,
Chased squirrels up the mountain,
Swam in the fast currents.

There's no trace now,
Only a memory, faint,
Along with the names long dead,
Whispered in a mountain breeze.

Ode to Cleopatra

Oh, Cleopatra, woman of firsts,
Woman of lasts,
You witnessed the beginnings,
And the ends of a civilization.

Oh, Cleopatra, woman of beauty,
Woman of wiles,
You beguiled the whims of those
Doomed; those briefly smelling Rome.

Oh, Cleopatra, woman of fortune,
Woman of fame,
You lifted your perfumed brow
To watch the fading sunset.

Oh, Cleopatra, woman so young,
Woman so full of life,
Your palace slipped into the sea
While the serpent's kiss put you to sleep.

Jack Trammell

When I Saw the Great Impressionists

When I saw the great Impressionists,
When I met Monet and Cassatt,
I saw the possibilities in colors and
Wondered at how they had lain
Hidden and undiscovered all those years.

Renior, Van Gogh, Manet and
All were masters of that vibrancy,
Welders of bold strokes and armed with brushes
Laden with pasty, cloud-like lightness.

When I saw the great Impressionists,
When I touched the felt of the unknown,
I savored the impossibilities and
Marveled at their complex simplicity,
Finally uncovered and discovered.

Emily

to Emily Dickinson

Emily
So lonely, so
Lovely and unlikely.
So shy,
Airy, aloof
Delighting in the light.

Jack Trammell

Reflections on Stalingrad

Men died:
half a million soviets
a quarter million nazis
But they weren't Soviets and Nazis
They were Men,
that's all.

The suffering was so great,
And the evil so deep
(as deep as the snow),
That ordinary soldiers performing
Ordinary tasks
Were suddenly angels sent from heaven.

And the historians keep saying,
"It was a great turning point!"
and crazy commies demand revenge
(shouting Marxist slogans at neo-facists),
But there was no significance apart from
Tragedy.

The lice were the winners
Until everyone died, and then
Even they froze.

In Moscow and Berlin
(and even in Washington D.C.)
Pins were pushed into places on a map,
Empty holes that even soldiers had
Abandoned to the winter;
To death's great Sixth Army.

Logic froze into madness;
Seige into mutual destruction, and even
cowards (what few there were) solidified into heroes.

Men died:
then the war continued
more tanks and guns
Fewer men,
Especially who knew how to fight.
Even those who survived, froze in camps.

Historians are the winners, the
Losers are still in the ice,
Testimony to insanity, complete and utter.

Jack Trammell

Grandma's Bread

A sense of place is important, even in this day and age of the Internet, subdivisions, superhighways, and growing pessimism. I was born in the western Appalachians, and live just east of them now. There is (I hope) a bit of that sense of place in all of my poems that anchors me to my identity and my home. My place is where my literary heroes hail from--Robert Penn Warren, Jesse Stuart, Wendell Berry--and is also home to those nameless kin who share all these stray thoughts and experiences in common with me.

This poem is for and about my Grandmother, one of the people my heroes wrote about.

I was a kid once, too
Grandma said,
Baking bread,
Rolling it out, working it out.
Lived in a log house
She said,
Face red,
Kneading it out, working it out.
Went to a one room school
She said,
Dough spread,
Pushing it out, patting it out.
Johnny Grammer, the teacher, was fun
She said,
Oven red,
Lifting it up, pushing it in.
And the girl who wouldn't stop talking
She said,

Baking bread,
Waiting it out, cleaning it up.
He'd get real mad and yell at her
She said,
Baking bread,
Pulling it out, cooling it off.
"Well hersh, cain't ya hersh?!"
She said,
Buttering bread,
Setting it out, smiling at it.

Jack Trammell

Yellow Rose
to Beatrice 1908-2000

Even silk flowers must eventually fade
Just as a favorite novel always has a final chapter.
Bea was our yellow rose, small and fragile,
Strong in so many hidden ways.

Quick to laugh, quick to smile,
Climbing stairs in life without complaint,
Reading daily between the lines and
Standing beside Russ at the corner store.

She knew the joy of daughter discovery;
The joy of growing grandchildren;
The joy in the quiet and silence;
The joy of goldfish ponds in the mind.

Even silk flowers must eventually fade
Just as the apple continually falls in Eden.
Bea was our yellow rose, witty and gentle,
Strong in so many ways.

Oasis

Desert air separates me from her,
A vast space filled with the nomadic people
who inhabit my daily doldrums.

Crossing each dune, I can see her clearly,
A vision of everything beautifully human;
bliss perfection that escapes description.

Cool water, trickling down the side of a glass
Cannot refresh the way a single glance at her
changes burning sands into glass.

In a universe so completely vast,
So baffling and utterly overwhelming,
is it possible that she might notice me?

Jack Trammell

Edgar Poe

From Boston he hailed
of Irish stock,
An actor's son with
orphan's frock,
A patron's name he carried to fame,
Fitting his fancy to life's short clock.

He started his journey
with Tamerlane,
Later the Raven
and Allan's blame,
Whose lack of support did not comport,
Budding brilliance oft called insane.

Through Richmond, Philadelphia,
and Baltimore,
Fate cast black shadows
he couldn't ignore,
The writer's quill he clinched with a will,
Sealing sadness in the name of Lenore.

The Father of Mystery,
the Inventor of Terror,
A lover of words
today so much rarer,
His time ticked so short, he found no support,
In the bottle bequeathing deep horror.

In the depths of his heart
he always stayed true,
Through all disappointment,

though melancholy grew,
He penned 'til the end and still tried to mend,
Burnt bridges he'd sundered in two.

His life was another
sad tale of woe,
He longed for a family
yet died all alone,
He kept Allan's name without any shame,
Anguished author, Edgar Allan Poe.

for a great Poe website go to: http://www.eapoe.org

Belle Isle
Audrie Miller & Jack Trammell

Belle Isle represents a team effort. Just as friendship can result in laughter and fun, it also can result in artistic synergy and creativity.

We found that the creation of this book led to many other wonderful discoveries, including some important individual realizations that will stay with us for a long time.

"Art is noisy," Audrie says, and I think this small book makes a lot of noise.

We hope you enjoy reading it as much as we enjoyed making it!

Audrie Miller is a 37-year-old central Virginia artist, mother of four, wife, and art teacher. She resides in Bumpass, Virginia.

Jack Trammell is a 38-year-old central Virginia writer, father of three, husband, and historical researcher. He resides in Bumpass, Virginia.

December 2002, Jack and Audrie
http://www.jacktrammellbooks.com

Dear Turkey, Happy Day

Dear Turkey, happy day. You make this day so special, how you may say? Your giblets flavor my sauces as mother in law, she bosses.

Pass the gravy it's so fine, I'm sneaking out for 99. (proof) I take a peek at the apple pie. Opps little Johnny shot out the dog's eye.

Flitter and fly; Bustle and bump. Hey! we cooked the festive pig's rump. Surrounded by glory and bright shining eyes, we hear uncle Ed's baseball story ...again. What a surprise!

My arms are sore and my face is a sweat. Will I be enjoying you chickie? Baby you bet.

So my Dear Mr. Turkey, thanks once again I'm sure we didn't give you of too much to complain.

Audrie Miller

Jack Trammell

Man is Born to Fish

Man is born to fish
(Peter opened his nets)
As birds are born to flight
(Jesus filled them).

The first time you catch
A native brook, bold
Spotted and iridescent,
Fragile and cold,

The first time you do it
With fly rod delight
Using a small brown fly,
Feeling the snap of a bite,

The first time you feel
Struggle and resistance,
In a pool of clear water,
Foam roaring intense,

The first time, you realize

Man is born to fish
("Very like a whale")
As horses are born to run
(Humbling in simple enormity).

Jack Trammell

Turkey Day 2, 3, 4, 5...

Okay Mr. Turkey is this some kind of a joke? Not just one day of feasting. Man you going for broke.

Turkey sandwiches and Turkey pie I'd knock you out if you had an eye. "Honey we must eat all of this bird. Don't you know starving children have heard?"

Turkey soup and turkey hash when can we throw your carcass in the trash?

"No not yet, still but one more dish. Have you ever tasted turkey broth with fish?"

"Smile dear it's good for you, so what if it tastes like Elmer's glue."

So once again, Mr. Turkey, it's been a fine tour but good grief!! Next year it's roast beef.

Audrie Miller

Audrie Miller, 2002

                                  "Your open hand
lifts
        me
                up."

Jack Trammell

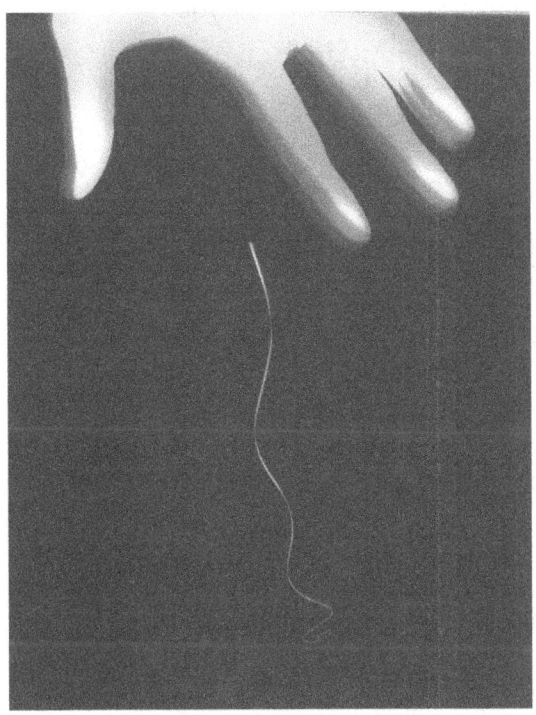

Hand Dropping Floss, photo, Audrie Miller, 2002

Jack Trammell

Beauty Fades

Although beauty fades as time invades,
Erasing youth in one swift poof!
We yet rely on that pumpkin pie (that we spy)
On the table so lush with goodness and calories!

Few things left to comfort the soul,
But filet mignon and that day old roll.
Maybe that's why they call it
    Middle Age Spread

Pass the butter.

Audrie Miller

Simple Riddle

A riddle to ponder
While my mind it does wander
Alone in my thoughts
Drinking stormy draughts
Of tearful tea

Audrie Miller

Jack Trammell

The Great Wall of Japan

The Great Wall of Japan
Came crashing down,
The Mongols somehow
Found their way to Richmond.

The Emperor's men (or women)
Were stunned, silent, and
Mom just kind of opened her mouth
And slowly stood up.

Everyone okay?
The Emperor (the cook) called,
A quick head count revealed
No one missing a head.

Reconstruction was swift, though
Mom still seemed consternated.
But then everyone laughed, and
Even the Emperor (cook) smiled.

The Great Wall of Japan
Had a small nick or two.
Our own army of comedians
Laughed out into the night.

Jack Trammell

Blue Days When the Sun Goes Down

I see the blue sky.
I see the sun go down.
And when the sky gets dark,
I know it's night.

I feel sleepy, and
I think about the stars.
I wonder if they are a shining glow?
I wonder if they know

I'm there.

I think the sky is just water.
I think I am getting very sleepy…

Hannah Trammell

P.S. My daddy typed this for me.

Hannah won first place in the state of Virginia for this poem. One might hope that it portends well for her writing aspirations!

Jack Trammell

Rhyming Game

Eyes blue, through and through,
She steals the sky and gives it to you.
Hair of flax, golden sun catch,
She steals the plot about to hatch.
Perfect nose, worthy of prose,
She steals the love of the reddest rose.
Brilliant mind, creative and kind,
She steals your heart and soul combined.
Vibrant smile, laughing with style,
She steals the distance from any mile.
Beautiful heart, a work of art,
She steals the time that's spent apart.

Appalachian Dreams

Mystery meat is good for the soul (every once in a while)

Auddie, Audrie Miller: "Art is noisy."

Jack Trammell

Dancer's New Song

1:         The waves are slowing to the rhythm of the
dancer's beat, and everything is quiet so the
heartbeats can show in a perfect manner.
We see a night in darkness and light.
We seek one so bright let his light show and
guide us through hard times, that maybe we
can be better people than we are now.

(Repeat)

Chorus: Dance to the lovely rhythm so
everyone can see the talent God has
given you and me.

2:         Sometimes it may be hard to show yourself but
in the end God will give you strength to do
what He planned for you.
So, do your best and show what you've got and help others be
confident to all who think just a thought about Jesus.

(Chorus)

Bethany Miller

Early Morning Light

January morning, velvet glow
Trees so thick they blur gray,
Except the oaks, who stubbornly
Cling to leaves like prideful boys.

There is a silence that clings,
Even in the age of technology,
Which refuses to leave until the
Sun burns it away into the blush.

Virginia pines brood, resinous
Green, dark, patient, so quiet;
Their bark is a curled scroll
Upon which squirrels busily compose.

I am the outsider, I think,
The one who decided this moment
To join in the celebration,
The one who must so swiftly leave.

Beauty remains unchanging, though, and
The cosmos must operate this way.
So early morning light was planned
On the first dawn of creation.

Jack Trammell

Jack Trammell

Hairy France

Oh, to live in hairy France,
    where no one laughs at underpants.
Where all is hair and love and wine,
    and shaggy eyebrows quite divine.

Oh, if only in hairy France,
    my forested legs would jig and dance,
Unabashedly so, with no remorse,
    As I joyfully devour each successive course.

Oh, hairy France, she calls to me,
    in night's dreamy cacophony,
In love and wine and heart's despair,
    where beauty waxers best beware.

Audrie Miller

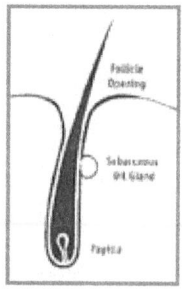

Season Change

Comes lightly, quietly,
Thieving the heat of dawn.
Crows cackle sharply,
Startled by the first yellow leaf.
Grass hugs heavy dew,
Golden rod falls amber wilting.
Loud summer storms dream into
Damp, slow, dripping showers.
Children's laughter, lost in
Schoolroom brightness and books.
Lovers part, temporarily,
Promises made, plans laid.
Change arrives, a wet traveler,
Quickly stands beside the warm fire.
Hangs coat and hat, tired,
Thankful to spend the night.

Jack Trammell

Kid Quotes

ALEC:

"Please get me some baby carrots! The French dip needs a friend."

(on Estes dining hall) "You should work here, Dad. You could cook and get PAID for it."

MADDIE:

"I've never been to North Carolina before. ('Yes you have!') I know, but not to socialize."

(on stratus clouds) "Those clouds don't need to go to the bathroom, do they?"

(on Cumberland, Maryland) "Hey, Cucumberland!"

"I don't like your bacteria tie." (my paisley tie)

(baseball play by play) "And Mike Piazza has hit another homerun! It's 100 to nothing!"

(on drinking liquids before bed) "It's okay, Dad. I don't have any trigger problems."
(Page 9)

(on the 2nd biggest wolf) "So he's the vice alpha male, right?"

(on why she's so talented) "It's because I have selective hearing, and I'm proud of it."

HANNAH:

"The moon is like a baseball that never hits the ground."

"Mommy, I smell a stunk."

"Daddy... The gargirls (gargoyles) are the good guys!"

"What are ferflections?" (reflections)

"Let's play Intendo." (Nintendo)

"That's ferdiculous." (ridiculous)

"These are pictures of the ray caverns." (Luray)

"Why is it snowing? It's already snowed this year."

MATTHEW: (Jack's nephew)

"Did you know Uncle John is like a child? He's stomping in the mud puddle. It's REE-DICK-U-LUSS! Now he's making Adam do it!!"

OTHER KIDS: (Touring the college)

('Do you know what Mr. Trammell does here at night?') "Clean up the floors and stuff?" (the answer was play basketball in the gym...)

Ode to Ned

Ned, Ned,
The metal horse head,
He's on the porch,
He's in the flowerbed.
Ned, Ned,
Rusty horse turned red,
He's in the washroom,
He's a friend he said.

Ned, Jack Trammell

Appalachian Dreams

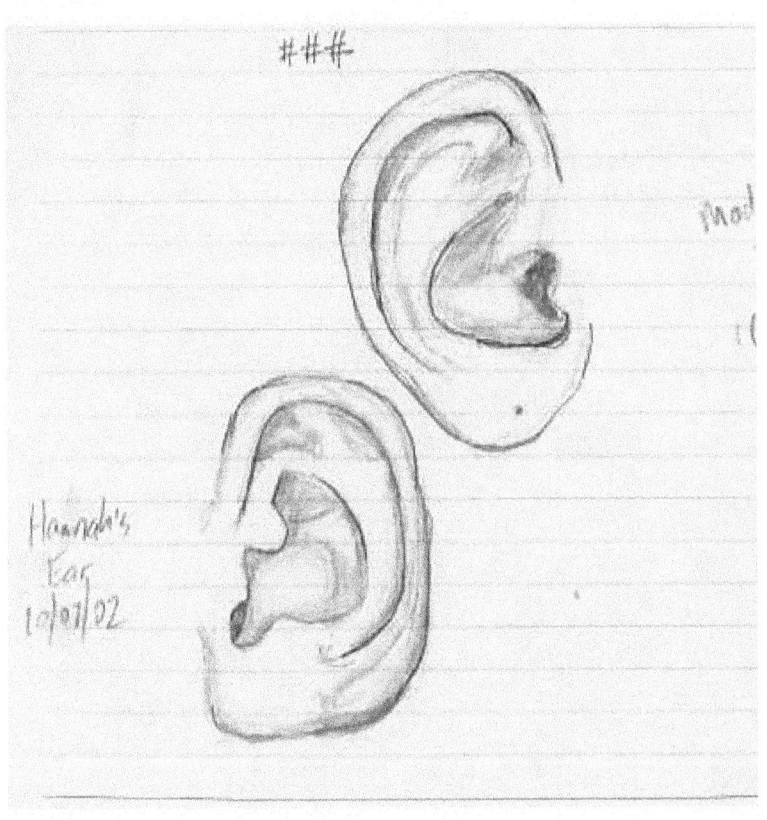

Maddie's and Hannah's Ears, Jack Trammell

Jack Trammell

Mrs. Greenhow

Who is Mrs. Greenhow?
She was a spy, who asked why,
Must I die with a load of gold
In my dress.
I must confess that I would weigh less
Without this gold in my dress.
My life will attest to no other contest
But to confess the misdeeds
Of the north and the west.

("And never the South!" *Jack*)

Audrie Miller

Mind of the Terrorist

I am blinded by hatred.
I hate your children, but
I love my offspring.
I hate your decadence, but
I cherish my extremism.
I hate your freedom, but
I prize my independence.
I hate your flag-waving, but
I value most my cause.
I am blinded by love.

Jack Trammell

Jack Trammell

Haiku

Sunny morning wakes
Allowing sadness to fade
I arise and smile.

Yellowed grasses fall
Carpets of glowing beauty
And wind sings alone.

Stacks of bricks tumble
Noisy drooling invasion
The dog is out now.

Crisp stuffy rustle
Highway vibration disturbs
Flat tire at midnight.

Audrie Miller

A New One...

A new one…
As day wasted, you remember,
One unseasonably hot day in September,
Where you wore on your sleeve
Your heart's sweat.

A bad idea realized one auction too late,
Where you found your lonely print
With some dog food next to a plate.

Your shame it does creep,
Redder necked than from sleep,
You awake to discover
In locale no willing art lover.

Audrie Miller

Discovery (Crabtree Falls at Night)

As the day turns into night,
And the hemlocks sleep from blight,
You will find without any fright,
How to finally live your delight,
Though recently you gave just a mite...

Jack Trammell and Audrie Miller

New Color

What if...

God made a new color
That no one could see?
I wonder exactly
What color it'd be...

Pigments turn black as night—
We call them "shades,"

We worship the sunlight
Though it's brightness that fades.

What if...

God made a new color
And nobody knew...
Might it be turquoise
That was bluer than blue?

Maybe it'd be orange
Much too vivid to see,

Or maybe, just maybe...
We've got all the colors we need.

Jack Trammell

(inspired by a Bill Nye video on light)

Jack Trammell

Boys Like Trains

Why is it that little boys like trains so much?
They're not like computers, or other toys as such.
But something about them makes every boy pause,
When the ground starts to tremble they look out, because,
Boys Like Trains.

The rattles and screeches that cut through the air,
If you're standing too close are almost too much to bear.
Some sounds are quite frightful; cause a skip of the heart,
Convincing, no doubt, the whole thing's falling apart, still
Boys Like Trains.

Colors aplenty, unique to train cars,
Ranging from rust red to black, sooty tar.
Bright yellow for Railbox, and bright green for NP,
Bright blue for Great Northern, dull gray for V & T,
Boys Like Trains.

Trains transport neat things, sometimes you can see,
Like trucks and containers, or cars and SUVs.
Hoppers spill out coal, or are dusty with grain,
Gondolas filled with scrap metal, rusty from rain,
Boys Like Trains.

Boxcars hide their contents, away in the dark,
Orange juice, computers, or even tree bark.
Tanks cars are dirty, even those painted black,
Inside of them milk, oil, or even shellac,
Boys Like Trains.

And when the train's gone, have you ever done this?
Jumped onto the tracks to see what you missed.
And as the tracks stretch away, and the last car is gone,
You sudden realize the conclusion I've drawn, is
Boys Like Trains.

Jack Trammell

Jack Trammell

Coming off the Mountain

Coming off the mountain
    Rain intensifies,
        Uncertain rocks stare upward,
            While truth hides deep wherein.

Walk slowly, you envoy of man,
    Your presence is noticed
        And the tree gods frown and glower
            Lamenting interrupted pavane.

Slipping and plodding down the trail
    An ant hopping along stupid,
        Purpose is left upon high summit
            Above the swirling gale.

Coming off the mountain,
    Sun abruptly pries clouds loose,
        Revelation is mind honey,
            Milk to nourish the free man.

Falling in Love (Again)

Once more, it arrives,
The tempest appears from beyond the shore,
Intrepid feelings disembark after too long
Cooped up inside inhibitions.

There is yet another New World, the
Alternate route to nowhere has been discovered,
Riches, glory, power, all the jewels of Coronado
Shine brightly so that one can see by their light.

It is fitting, however, that the journey be recognized,
Altogether appropriate that history repeats itself, again
Fools or no, the inevitability of it is trite, but true,
Though the rocks wait ominously, patiently.

Falling in love again is to board the ship,
Before the storm has quenched its anger.
Forgetting to reef the sails, risking the masts,
To damn the hurricane's fury with a smile.

The channel is narrow, nary a living man can
Say he knows its path for certain;
No earthly philosophy can explain its depths or
Shallows, or tack into its sharpest gusts.

So many fools (or are they just wise?)
Thirst for the adventure, yearn for the danger,
Ready to die for the possibility of a single drop,
A tiny happiness, fall in love, again.

Jack Trammell

Jack Trammell

Fernandina Beach

Stretches like light
A fossil of the moment,
Wind in constant dance
With the stillness.

Each wave is an opportunity
To see something else,
Each living sand dollar
The finger tip of another wave.
Black, shiny shark's teeth
Litter the sand for the curious,
Cheerful gulls fly backwards
In leeward breezes.

Fills your senses with passion
Your eyes with music,
Ocean gray pulls at the limits of
Inner sanctum of soul imagination.

Jack Trammell

Child's Question

What if there is no heaven?
My daughter inquired of me.
If we never see great grandma again,
Exactly what would that really mean?

I guess we all seek a sign, I said,
An assurance that faith is form.
A sacred balm, given freely to all,
But especially to those who mourn.

I told her that people simply can't see
The things that we love the most.
And heaven, the biggest one of them all,
Though seemingly it should be so close.

By the look on her face I saw I'd failed,
Her expression told me quite clearly.
A child's question then becomes the adults',
An answer we long for so dearly.

Jack Trammell

Rising Action

Your open hand
                lifts
                me
                up.

Your open heart
                fills
                me
                up.

Your soft arm
                picks
                me
                up.

Your open mind
                thrills
                me
                up.

Jack Trammell

Asklepios

Is Dead.
But the sacred waters
Still heal,
Braziers still broil, the
Paean is still sung.
Mythic shadows still flicker,
Ἰεϱοί λόγοι
Hum in common dreams,
History only half-complete.

Jack Trammell

List 03/19/02 at Urkops

Pick up some milk   the life I've built
And get some bread   I sometimes dread
Get some TP   others can't see
Dog food, cat food   so why seem rude?

Diet Pepsi   they miss the key
Maybe orange juice   one nut too loose
Shampoo, razors   I hate all stores
The newspaper   time is a blur.

Jack Trammell

Mission on Three Ridges

I found the trail in mist and rain,
    I pulled my cinch straps tight.
Motivation was hard to explain,
    Meaning was seemingly slight.

Through a meadow the metaphor first rose from,
    The trees started slowly to speak.
Each leaf with shimmering pitter-patter drums,
    Each droplet a small melting peak.

The message was clear, the meaning complete,
    Certainty rose in the fog clouds.
My smallness was real, wafting up in the heat,
    As the morning evolved into sounds.

Three Ridges in legend as well as real life,
    Mountains defy elevation.
Sucking thin air and breathing my tithe,
    Pale rocks God's sharp revelation.

Jack Trammell

Jack Trammell

Waking Up By the River

Murm'ring water,
Last sound discerned, first sound returned,

Dreams fade to blur.

Cupid's daughter,
Lately adjourned, still to be yearned,

Passion will stir.

Ner' you've caught her,
Though desire burned, pounding heart churned,

To reason demur.

Whisp'ring water,
Logic spurned, wants to be earned,

Patience! love her.

Jack Trammell

The Heart!

My heart is going "Thump, thump, thump!"
It seems not to faint.
It looks like I can give up now.
It never goes away!

Maddie Trammell

That Faraway Place

That faraway place
That I'm looking for
Is often right beside me.
That distant Eden
Dreamed in dreams
Is frequently close at hand.
That promised land
Between bubbling brooks
Is tumbling ever closer.
That nameless mist
That poets call love
Is swirling so close at hand

Jack Trammell

By the Laughing Ocean

By the laughing ocean,
God's bewitching beauty
Gazes soul ward,
Blooming enchanted
Bouquet.

Jack Trammell

Summer Storm

One hot summer day four children were on a boat. Their names were Krystal, Jessica, Luke, and Daniel.

"This is boring," said Luke.

"Let's go to the snack bar," said Daniel.

So all four walked to the snack bar. When they got back Jessica couldn't help but to say, "The sky looks threatening."

"We can see that," said the three others, sarcastically.

But suddenly it started to rain! The water came higher and higher up until the boat tipper over!

"I forgot how to swim!" gasped Krystal.

"That's so cheap," said the three others.

All night they swam in the ocean. In the morning they saw that they got washed up on an island!

"Where are we?" yawned Krystal.

(TO BE CONTINUED)

Mary Claire Miller

Sleepless in Bumpass

Sleepless in Bumpass,
Dreams for strangeness surpass,
Bad guys the good guys lambaste,
Til finally, you wake up at last.

Jack Trammell

Coffee House Blues

He made a science of the aromas, attempting to draw comparisons that had never been imagined. Espresso was molasses with the sugar removed; au lait was the smell of a white rose after it was cut and wilted in the hot sun; Columbian supreme was a bitter, bitter chocolate, distilled over and over again to blackness.

He sat in the shop often, sometimes reading books and magazines donated by people who had found more interesting things to read, sometimes writing poems on the side of the napkin underneath his coffee mug, but always smelling the smells.

Decaf had a weak, nut-like odor, detectable a mile away; French vanilla dripped with the air of a German confectionary shop (and it did not occur to him odd at all to use those two countries in the same comparison).

There was a day after he had become quite adept at his olfactory exercises that his car stopped running, abandoning him on the side of the highway, and it was a natural thing for him to briskly walk the two or three blocks to the coffee shop while the vehicle was being repaired.

He ordered a latte, extra strong, and sat down in his favorite ladder-back chair to savor the smell.

To his complete and utter shock, a new odor abruptly invaded his nostrils, stealing his comfiture as rudely as a child taking another's toy.

It was a combination of pink lemonade with too much sugar, and the smell of soft skin immediately after a hot, soapy shower. It was an odor he had never encountered before.

He rose slowly, almost automated, to follow the smell; to study it, describe it, and catalog it. He left the steaming, frothy latte on the round glass table beside the ladder-back chair where it soon grew quite cold, and was swept back to the kitchen and poured down the drain.

The smells of coffee did not follow him out the door.

Jack Trammell

Jack Trammell

"Tracks", Audrie Miller

Prayer #1

Pray that what might be, will be,
And that what was and has been
Will be known.
Ask for the impossible with no fear,
And ask for what is simple and good,
What will be known.
Amen.

Jack Trammell

Reminder

TOMORROW'S lunch is cabbage soup and the last day of school is Monday 3, 2002. Maria Payne, Jenny Whitaker, Kathy Parter, Robert Keen and Mary Jacobs can come to the office to receive their birthday stickers from the office. Today's lunch is stuffed crust pizza. Brittany Kacy and John Bearable are the attendance winners today. Carrie Shiftlit and Barbra Henson need to talk to the principal about the food fight they started.

Also...Kim Needy is food poisoned by the lunch lady and Poopdeck Pappy wet his pants yesterday. Barney Gappy ----ed in the lunch lady's face. Everyone who ate yesterday's lunch will report for a heart scan and 5th grade is having a field trip to Clappiesville...

...Now join me in the school song...

Bethany Miller

Hannah, My Hannah

My youngest,
My most vulnerable.
My own selfishness
Pales next to the life
You haven't yet led.

God has not given me
More than two hands
And a head to protect you,
So I pray for something more
To guard your precious smile.

I'm losing faith in the world
(not in God, you must understand)
But as God is ever-present
So I must be too,
Watching Hannah, my Hannah.

Jack Trammell

"Heaven might be like a model train layout where the train never comes back to the same place."

(Jack answering a question from Hannah)

Jack Trammell

Drunken Fella

Drunken fella

Mia bella, ona staira

Breaka danca

In underweara

Falla downa

Feela clowna

Go to bed in wifa's gowna

Waka upa

Drink a cupa

Down the draino

Looks like raino.

Audrie Miller

Appalachian Dreams

"Untitled", *Christopher Miller*

Jack Trammell

"Mary Claire and Christopher", Mary Claire Miller

"Max"

From Amos to Audrie

For three sins,
    Even for four
I would not turn my back on you.
Do two people walk together
Without agreeing to do so?

For three sins,
    Even for four
Some would sell the righteous for silver.
But I would I raise you up to be my queen
Would you not want it so?

For three sins,
    Even for four
A hand that draws the plumb line falters.
But I would I stagger to you
Return from the bottom of the sea.

For three sins,
    Even for four
Some would mend the broken places.
Do two people walk together
Without embracing those places?

Jack Trammell

Before Me

The mountain was here
    Before me...
Piles of sliding shale stone,
Old trails leading to hidden traces,
Gnarled chestnut oaks praying for sun,
    Before me.
Before the world reached in
And plucked me out,
Before the road was paved
With strange notions of progress.

This hollow was here
    Before me...
Shadows of trees long gone,
Mingle with white-tailed deer.
Scarlet flower secrets revealed,
    Before me.
Before my own anxiety trapped me
In existentialist torment,
Before electric lights divided
This side from that one.

This house was here
    Before me...
White clapboard over roughed timbers,
Tin roof from a rolling mill far away,
Wavy glass eyes overlooking high pasture,
    Before me.
Before I turned inside out
And forgot who I really am,
Before I turned and chased a shadow
And found myself before the mountain.

Trial and Error

Lithium?
Or lots of love, who's the one to say...
Lots of Praise?
Or punishment, likely both, either way...
A little Xanax?
Or some Xanadu, just around the bend...
A few more rules?
Or more rushed speech, grace that cannot end...
Broken glass?
Or a broken heart, one is more replaceable.
Yelling, loud?
Or absolute silence, either is erasable.
On camera?
Or off camera, always one new drama...
Alcohol?
Or Starbuck's, just drink away the trauma...
Go with sleep?
Or go without sleep, twenty-four is straight...
Make it hot?
Or make it cold, make it always late...
Brilliant today?
Or totally sluggish, who's the one to say...
A little Prozac?
Or a little prosaic, likely both, either way...

(inspired by Jean Lancaster's Short Story about BPD)

Jack Trammell

Lament #7

Hurt clings like a needy woman,
Pulling hardest as you step away…
Pleading for a fleeting mercy
Over which the intellect holds no sway.

Hers' is such a plain entreaty,
A simple message for every day…
She will not break her gaze from you,
Or allow you to rush on your way.

Are you still there??

We're here, you and me,
You reading and me writing.

Connected through ink and paper,
Letters and words,
Ideas and instincts.

But I really have no control
When you will stop,
When I will stop,
When that moment will occur
Where something makes sense
Or you suddenly are bored
And toss this away.

Ascribe it to poetry, or
Constant sea roar of language,

Forever is a gift we share
As long as your eyes linger
Where my pen gathers chaos
Into small patterns of eternity.

Sin, failure, and success,
Just words for a bad sermon.
Unless you are there…

Love, trust, and longing,
Just bad Hallmark cards.
Unless you are there…

And I am here,
Telling you point-blank,
I am lonely.

Are you still there?

Jack Trammell

My Gift to You

My gift to you, like Alec on guitar:
Loud, fun and just a little out of control…
My gift to you, like Maddie in goal:
Lean, fast, and just a little out of control…
My gift to you, like Hannah's book soul:
Learned, factual, and just a little bit bizarre…

My gift to you, all three of you, my only treasure,
Is a wealth safe from threats, beyond all measure.

Before I bequeath it, before I expound,
Bear with me a moment, the reasons you should care:
You may not like the clothes, the bright ties that I wear;
My weird friends might sometimes give you a scare;
You might not always think I act quite fair;
But my reasons for gifting you are indeed quite sound.

My gift to you will not expire; and best of all,
Though small in size, it's a really big haul.

My gift to you, Alec, for all your horseplay:
The way you smile when you're in trouble;
Your quiet moods with intensity so subtle;
The way you work and give it double;
Your kid-like smile with three-day-old stubble;
My gift to you, Alec, needs no repay.

My gift to you will not expire; and best of all,
Though not as big as you, it is not small.

My gift to you, Madeline, for all your mischief:
The way you care for those around you;
Your awesomeness award is long overdue;
The way you work and always come through;
Your impish smile that you never outgrew;
My gift to you, Maddie, will give you a lift.

My gift to you will not expire; and best of all,
It's filled with thrills and a curtain call.

My gift to you, Hannah, for all of your brains:
The way you create those literary only-ifs;
Your awesome song lyrics and deep poetical riffs;
The way you create those "silent deadly look" tiffs;
Your expressions those wonderful facial hieroglyphs;
My gift to you, Hannah, always remains.

My gift to you three will not expire; and best of all,
It's my love for you, beyond all recall.

Jack Trammell

The Poe Syndrome (journal entry dated 1841)

You feel that everyone must understand, or
Doesn't understand
But must understand
You.

Yet
You don't understand you.

You write these lines
These LINES   H E R E

But they still don't understand.
They call you sick.
They call you morbid.
Drunkard. Thinker
Of foul secrets and dead souls.
Forecaster of disaster,
Foreteller of Hell, Ur and Sodom.

They must understand.
They must.

If I write these lines
These WORDS   H E R E

They must understand!

I must tell them,
Must let them know, somehow!
That I know,
That it is morbid.

It is from hell.
It is not a forecast but a
State of being.

You must understand!!

Birds and Bees

There comes a time when parents know
They must sit down and have the talk,
Smile adult smiles, try not to balk,
And above all else nerves must not show.
Regal import they must bestow:
No interruptions, no loud squawk,
If pictures used they must not gawk,
Only somber frowns apropos.

It won't last long, that's what they say,
But they were people without grace,
Without a clue why to obey,
Rules simply to avoid disgrace.
But you and I, these birds are ours…
Don't forget why bees love flowers.

Sweet Sun Rays

Sweet sunshine of my memory,
How my fingers ache for your
Warm earthen touch.

My wife, sleeping sublime,
Warm summer nights;
Snuggle in winter covers;
Nap beside on golden fall winds.

But you, Helios, I must endure separation from,
Year after year, our Winter Solstice divorce.

The bed I share with you warms only slowly…

I plow your fallow covers over to await you,
Patient as
Snow melts.
Your chirping retinue sings in preparation,
Slender stalks bend over in obeisance
        (waiting)
Air begins to hum,
Even deer hold their ears up,
Expecting you any moment.

Sweet sun rays, remind me,
Remind me again
You haven't forgotten our seed,
You will come back
        (I'm waiting)

The promise we made each other.

Jack Trammell

Marsh Creek

Between two mountains
Along a pathway
Beside the deer-lick
Hidden in shadow
Birthplace of father
Lowland and farmhouse
Shadow of purple
Below the white-oaks
Along the frontier
Between two mountains
Framing the limestone
Sacred to native
Hiding the black-bear
Silent the schoolhouse
Eroded the gravestones
Crystal the water
Crumbling a well-house
Restless a hoot-owl
Between two mountains

(Marsh Creek is along the Tennessee/Kentucky border and home to generations of the author's family)

A Shape I Wist

What's this I see? A shape I wist!
One more book with a vampire plot,
With lots of blood that will not clot,
I've had enough—cease and desist!
Bats, fangs, werewolves, I get the gist!
A tad more class would hit the spot,
Sometimes even a Gordian knot,
Please, not the love triangle twist!

Oh, for some genuine real fear,
A black shadow without substance,
Or a villain that makes dark sense,
A true hero to persevere…
But this shape I wist doth consist
Of its own monster in our midst.

(inspired by Coleridge—a little bit…)

Jack Trammell

Portrait of a Shipwreck

Divining rods,
Alchemist's science or
Amazement for step-son?

I take long lost art,
Make blustery January
Beach adventure.

The rods cross here;
X marks the spot,
Don't step on our marks!
(with your dog-walking indifference…)

Slowly, like an old story,
Outline takes shape,
A fifty foot keel revealed.

Remains of a ship!
No other object in nature
Curves that important way.

Blockade runner?
17th century pirate?
Hurricane driven fishermen?

Picture perfect,
Our discovery, only lines in sand,
Picture perfect.

"We found a shipwreck!"
His look, worth a little bit of divorce,
Worth the cold.

That old history teacher:
Not so crazy after all,
Could probably tell us what ship it is.

Jack Trammell

Diversity

A city on a hill,
Where none of us live.

But we know someone else there.

And we want to live there.

Portrait of A.

She is like the road near
Where my mother was born:
Winding,
Dusty,
Smiling,
Promising.

Her hair falls over an eye
(lucky eye)
I blush inside my excitement.

She could not be less or more,
Perfect.
I see only similitudes,
Visions of love,
Waiting around each corner.

Her pause is a smile
(lucky lips)
I want to rush and embrace her.

She could not be less or more,
Exactly.
I see only my dreams reflected,
Dreams of romance,
Dancing near a crystal lake.

She is like the cabin near
Where my mother was born:
Simple,
Inviting,
Unpresupposing,
Promising.

Jack Trammell

Jack's Bad Day

There once was a Falcons fan,
Who was such a very sad man,
Though he screamed and he flailed,
The evil Packers prevailed;
Another season was thrown in the can.

Spider

Black Widow,
Curled under fungus-wood,
Cold, motionless toy.

A poke elicits only
Further curling, only
Barest of responses.

Outside the woodshed,
Winter stalks the air,
Reaching inside the rafters.

Inside the season
Nature sleeps, and
I can't stir her.

Another Battle

Mall or field? Intruder or shield?
Bayonets and muskets are now
Web pages and press releases.
The cause is just and noble:
"Hold on to the past!"
Yet who can capture the wind, and
Leave history just to the story-tellers?
Who can say how much is enough
When memory always flees?
Wal-Mart or trees? Saviors or thieves?
Cannon and bridles are now
Movies and Museum zoos:
"Hold onto the past!"
Yet how much is enough, and
When should the dead finally lie undisturbed?

Garden Haiku

Tiny Carmen button   (lady bug)
Creeping, crawling, crazy spots
Pause, as if frozen

Twisted flower vine   (on morning glory)
So purple royal silken white,
Despised by gardener

Companion to peas   (pea pod gaze)
Green harbinger of freshness:
Creation cries joy

Jack Trammell

Lucky

Lucky ain't lucky anymore
He didn't feel those eighteen wheels
Didn't hear the engine roar...
No, Lucky ain't lucky anymore

Smiley ain't smiley anymore
He stared him down he traded frowns
That biker couldn't ignore...
No, Smiley ain't smiley anymore

Frisky ain't frisky anymore
That old pit bull began to drool
That 9th live was no more...
No, Frisky ain't frisky anymore

Jolly ain't jolly anymore
He laughed his last he went so fast
Didn't even make it to the door...
No, Jolly ain't jolly anymore

Sorry ain't sorry anymore
What's done is done and fun is fun
We've evened up the score...
No, Sorry ain't sorry anymore

Now Singing, ain't singing any more
It's gone on too long for any song
It starts to be a bore...
No, singing ain't singing anymore

Jack Trammell and Audrie Miller

1990 and The Promise

Was this the promise faithfully awaited?
Was this the time when all good men rise up?
On ventilators their breath was bated
Chant "one of us" heave ho and raise the cup.

No pity sought by father Justin Dart,
Harkin's guidance a thousand ships sailed
On wings of hope from every brothers' heart
At last, arrived, at last justice prevailed.

Walking, seeing, hearing, learning, caring
Acts of major living forging ahead,
Hoyer's plotting nothing short of daring
Robert's dream for which many have bled.

It passed, its law! And ignorance retreats!
Alas, true battle remains on the streets.

(the author teaches classes related to the Disability Rights Movement and the ADA)

Poet's Advice

Be careful of the words you use,
    Be cautious of their pricks;
Words, like friends, with caution choose
    Lest they burn too close to wick.
With words you speak and words you write
    You lay your heart out bare;
But once released they take to flight,
    Where they land you're unaware…

Loss

I wish I could live
Between dreams and falling awake,
That place between the lie
And the reality
That lasts but a moment
Before depression grips.
That moment when mourning
Sunshine is an emotion
Rather than physical sensation;
That moment when the bed is
Neither empty nor filled—
    --just warm;
That moment when the interior
Rules the exterior
With fierce caring;
That moment before eyes
    --open
Naked before loss.

Jack Trammell

The Zebra Finch Revolt

Too loud!
Had to move them,
Out of the bedroom:
Little baby squawking,
Busy mom chirping,
Proud dad trolling male song.
Good grief, that's loud!

(Finally!)
(Had to alert them somehow)
(Get them somehow to notice:)
(Too cold in here,)
(Too close to them,)
(Too much talking noise.)
(Thank goodness, finally!)

Old House

This old house needs its ghosts,
Needs reminders that:
Life was hard (still is);
Marriage was difficult (still is);
Children grow up (still do);
That the sun will come up again,
Sneaking between old curtain and window frame,
Warming clapboard siding, and,
Eventually, a man and a woman in a bed.
Just like always.

Every creak, every loose board
A whisper of a memory
No one else recorded;
Every single square nail silently
Holding human lives contained.

Over decades, over centuries
The people come and go…

But this old house loves its ghosts,
Its walls embryos for warm life
(though not always for warm air…)

For those whom fate stopped on the road,
The crooked "for sale" sign
Suddenly bright red and unusually large.

Jack Trammell

Life of the Poet

Always something to say,
A sound, a shape, a song
The Muse inside holds sway.

The paper is the clay,
The feeling must be strong
Always something to say.

Words blossom a bouquet,
The heart is never wrong,
The Muse inside holds sway.

Novels fine; letters okay,
Feeling poets toil long,
Always something to say.

From One's Self do not stray,
To the craft you belong,
The Muse inside holds sway.

A poem starts the day,
A poem says so long,
Always something to say,
The Muse inside holds sway.

The Miller's Wife
(A poddle, or a poem that is also a riddle)

The miller's wife walked to the market,
    her bag was filled with flour.
On the shelves she found:
    a glower;
    an hour:
    and a dower.
She traded her flour for an hour
(and five loaves of bread)
While the dower and the glower
    Quickly ran away.

(There were three women in the market)

Jack Trammell

Get There

1. Well there's cars,
And there's bars,
And there's the kind of wheels that won't get you too far,
Depends on the ride and when you decide
How much you want that beer,
You should have just hit that deer...

Jack up the truck,
Call it bad luck.
Or call it good fortune it wasn't a big buck,
Swap on the spare and you're almost there
Remembering that the journey,
Is never guaranteed...

And every little bit that you can do to get you there,
Without the hoopla, and without fanfare,
Whatever slides you just a little bit closer,
Closer and closer to the next detour;

Just put one foot down and take the next step,
Walking forward is the only thing left,
And every little bit that you can do,
It gets you ready for the next snafu.

2. Late to work,
    Your boss a jerk,
    And there's never a good reason why he goes beserk,
    Depend on the check, the pain in the neck,
    Counting the seconds around the clock,
    While he's watching you like a croc...

Then you're home,
You hear the phone,
Soccer trip is leaving now and you chaperone,
There's never a time, it's always nickel and dime,
Gotta take a break somewhere along the line,
But now you're driving its too late to decline…

And every little bit that you can do to get you there,
Without the hoopla, and without fanfare,
Whatever slides you just a little bit closer,
Closer and closer to the next detour;

Just put one foot down and take the next step,
Walking forward is the only thing left,
And every minute longer you can survive,
At least confirms that you're still alive.

3. The day is done,
   The war is won,
   No other bad guy left you've got to outgun,
   At last you can stop, get off the clock,
   Put tomorrow with a shot on the rocks,
   Fall on the couch and pull off your socks.

   Then there's a sound,
   You look around,
   And it's right back onto the merry-go-round,
   Someone's awake—never a break,

Jack Trammell

Romania

Tuica plum rose aftertaste of Otherness;

Sun rises slowly over Carpathian contradiction:
Light and dark,
West and east,
Rational and irrational.

Cold, bitter ice, in winter's nest of worries,
Washed away by a smile and a laugh.
There can be no Revolution where there
Is no princess or a ploughman.

Dracula's blood-stained past is a
Hero's epithet, worn like a badge
By those who ignore Hollywood and
Would stay away from any crossroads.

New and old,
Hot and cold,
Real and surreal,
The sun sets on silent shrines and orthodox chapels.

My DNA does not lie:
Lamb stew and mint smell of the night.

The End

Divorce feels like the
Last bite of a
Tiny candy bar.
Appetite left hanging, though

There's nothing left.

Just a plastic crinkle,
A visual search for the trash can,
A whispering smudge on the chin,
A memory on the tip of the tongue.

Then it's gone.

The ecstasy evaporated;
The joy logged off;
An email address that doesn't work anymore;
Children gazing upward.

Just an empty wrapper
Slowly…
Slowly…
Unfolding in the trash can.

Who is Frank? Why is he friending me?

Frank…

Jack Trammell

Psalm #231

On the seventh day he left,
High road to Jericho
Nothing but the guilt on his back.

And on the third night he dreamt,
Camels, Kings, Saviors and Saints,
Dreamt of a time that might come.

But when he woke,
Embers dying and
Sunrise calling:

Three hungry mouths;
Three angry, sullen children;
A crowd with stones.

Then there was the mountain…

No choice, but Jericho-bound.

Prayer #15

Oh, Great Spirit in the Sky,
How do you keep track of us all?
How do you feel every hangover,
Know every pain,
Watch over every man studying an ant…
Must you delegate?

Perhaps an angel to watch the man
And the ant;
While you tend to a war, or a birth,

But how do you do it, Great Spirit?
I must know, in part because
I look at the ant; I look in the mirror,
I don't understand.

Jack Trammell

Cantos XVII

The bombs speak at their interview of
Weeping maidens for whom war is not kind.
Are they sad? I am.
Are they fearful? So I am.
All is fair, and fair are all who
Blush alive before the impact.

My God! My God! Why have you
Sent this rain of falling angels to
Water the children?

For Christ's sake!

Afghanistan, landscape of camouflaged
Tents, mystery caves and sullen muftis.
Misery stalks her shadows,
Madness dozes lightly, and
There is no president
No lunatic
No diplomat
With enough smoking guns or
Enough spit-flaming vitriol
To stem the creeping madness.

The bombs do not forget.
They lay in gritty memory-ground,
Partially buried in arms and legs
Once attached to real human beings.

If you bombs could cry, would your tears warn?
Would your summons announce in

Falsetto choral warnings,
Madness! Crouching madness...

They fall so silently,
Swimming mushrooms that blossom
Without sound,
Without voice.

The bombs finish their interview and leave
(what else would they do??)
The dead to bury the dead.

Jack Trammell

Aging

Aging is like waking up and really
Wanting to go back to bed;
But knowing that you can't.

It has no future tense;
Always steals the time unnoticed,
Bringing sudden awkward moments one can't befriend.

Will not drink with you,
Will not go to bed with you,
Instead just teases you.

Leaves you right when you want to ask
"What the hell are you talking about?"
Or "At least tell me what's next."

A wrinkle in time is a wrinkled line
A bad punch line with morning breath and
I want to go back to bed.

Getting old has no future, or
At least it has a past that's too far,
No diet can save.

So maybe aging is for wine or cheese—
But bullshit! It is NOT for me.

Trackside

Sound of speed transfixed
Silver blur leaves vacuum breath
Silent trackside void.

Idea of speed
Influence logic's new train
Innovation wheels.

Suspended belief
Sudden notion arrival
Slow discover—time.

Jack Trammell

The Fight

Occurred one day
Out in the blue, where
Clouds and ether normally hold sway.
Instead this day
Things turned black, when
Angst and anger had their way.
Wasn't worth it
Not even sure how
Neither one of us could admit.
Couldn't stop it
And I don't even know why
The thing matters not a bit.

I'm sorry…

As long as you're sorry.

About Christmas

Children make the holiday
>No matter what their age;
Children are the raison d'être
>Released from school's December cage.

Children, indeed, make the season
>In spite of what the adults do;
Children really need no reason
>To behave like everything's new.

The young ones are the happy ones
>Reminding us of youth;
The young ones are the angel suns
>Whose smiles will tell the truth.

Jack Trammell

Appalachian Dreams

www.ingramcontent.com/pod-product-compliance
Lightning Source LLC
Chambersburg PA
CBHW060524100426
42743CB00009B/1424